#FitToBeWilliamson

#FitToBeWilliamson

Tiffany Williamson

XULON PRESS

Xulon Press
2301 Lucien Way #415
Maitland, FL 32751
407.339.4217
www.xulonpress.com

Paperback ISBN-13: 978-1-6628-1907-0
Ebook ISBN-13: 978-1-6628-1908-7

TABLE OF CONTENTS

INTRODUCTION

Growing up, I thought everyone's father sold drugs. There was never a time I believed he was something else. My parents never hid it from me or my brothers, but with the drugs came the fights, lies and the women. After 17 years my parents got a divorce but from years of abuse suffered at the hands of my father, my mother was left with severe PTSD, which I believed was why she began to abuse me. I was completely unaware that one's mother was not supposed to beat you or smack you across the face because you may have looked at her wrong.

My mother took beatings to a whole new level. She would pick up anything close to her and knock you out. My mother would make plates fly across the room in a blink of an eye. One of the reasons I continued to help my mother even though she abused me mentally, verbally, and physically, was that she suffered from seizures. My guess is from a genetic disorder that was not discovered to be in the family until my daughter was born. My brothers all suffered the same abuse from our mother—the only difference is she stopped when they were teenagers. My mother never stopped with me. I continued to be abused by my mother up until I was thirty-eight years old. Easter 2020 was a powerful day for me, but I had been building up for this moment my whole life. And it was my time.

Chapter 1

THE EARLY YEARS

My dad was Thurston Johnson. He was also "Kiss." Kiss was a street pharmacist and Thurston worked on the military base. My dad would sell to everyone, including cops. Having friends in high places helped him out from time to time. I remember going to hotels by truck stops as a kid. My mom later told me its where he would get his shipments from. Towards the end of my parents' marriage Kiss was around more often. You see, he was two different people. My older brothers got the good guy, the guy who coached little league, organized fishing trips, spent holiday dinners at his mother's, and smiled in family pictures. My little brother and I saw the drug dealer. We saw him beating our mother to the point I was afraid to touch her. I remember one time she dyed her hair blonde and the blood turned it red. The mom I remember was always crying around this time. There was no joy in her face. I felt all her pain and I wanted to make her feel better. So, I would write letters to my mother and slide them under the door. At times, my mother would participate. My mother loved my father so much, but the drugs had a hold of my dad and there was nothing anyone could do. Not even my brothers could save our father.

I wonder if my brothers were confused. How could a man you looked up to, someone that you admired—a hero—suddenly turn into a man who delivered nothing but hate? My dad beat the hell out of my mom. Everybody knew, but no one cared. She eventually got sick of the lies, cheating, and fights. And she left, but she did so with little to no plan. My mother had the strength to leave my father, but she never learned how to survive without him. She tried replacing him, but no one could make her happy. She would have plenty of male friends, but she never really kept a boyfriend for long. Her mental state changed and she became incredibly angry. She would get mad over the smallest things. We would be afraid to be in the same room with her at times. After she broke away from our father. The man that beat the living crap out of her, she begins to beat the living crap out of her kids, especially me.

I got my first bloody nose at the age of seven. I was in my closet and it was a mess, which must have triggered her because she smacked me so hard in my face. It later became routine. Not only did she do it, but all four of my brothers would beat me as well. Do not get me wrong; as I got older, I started fighting back. The kids in the neighborhood would talk about how their mothers would whip them, so to my understanding this was completely normal.

Sixth grade was the most difficult year for me. We were going to be homeless soon, so we moved in with a family my mother knew. I had to babysit for the family while they went out to clubs and the horse races with my mom. They had twin boys who were about three and a five-year-old daughter. They were fun and well behaved. Their mom beat them as well, so I would make sure they had fun while I had them. We would play all kind of games, and for the night we ate like kings and queens. Mainly junk, but it was fun.

One morning my stomach was hurting so badly, but I had to go to school. Before first period I went to the restroom, and there was my first period. I had no clue what to do. I mean, I'd seen the health videos, but my mother never talked to me about anything pertaining to the female body. Now there I was with blood in my panties. I grabbed some toilet paper, rolled it up, shoved it in between my legs and went to class. I keep this up for a few months. My mother saw my panties but never questioned me. Looking back, I am still confused at why my mother never brought me pads. Was it my fault because I never told her? I mean, I never had a doctor growing up. If we got hurt, it was the ER. Soon after my Aunt Flow was well under way, mom mother got great news: a new job and a new home. My mother's job was right around the corner from our new home. The house was yellow with two rooms on the ground floor and one room, the master, above the garage. This was my favorite home. This is where I grew up, where I had my first kiss, and where the abuse got worse.

Living in Del City, Oklahoma, was Intense to say the least. Right before we moved into our own home, I sold a lot of candy for the school I was attending. I remember walking back to the house with two huge boxes. I had to have people help me because there was no way this sixth grader could carry so much candy. I got to the house and our stuff was packed and ready to go. My mom said,

"Well, we're not going to deliver all this." My mom put the boxes in the car, and we were off. After one week it was clear my mother did not plan again, as usual. Here we were in this house with no furniture, no gas, and no food. My brother and I froze our butts off. One thing we did have was the fundraiser candy. All I have to say is I hate peanut brittle, chocolate cover cherries and caramel or cheddar popcorn to this day. I am sure that helped with my type 2 diabetes.

Eventually my mom got some help through the government. She would receive food stamps, but nothing else. I remember the kids would talk about going to the dentist, and in my mind I thought they must have been rich. How could their mothers afford to take them to the dentist just for a cleaning? In my mind you only went to see the professionals when something was wrong, so for these kids to be going to the dentist just for a cleaning was crazy in my world. This behavior is passed down from generation to generation. At twelve and thirteen, I started to question a lot of things my mother was doing.

One thing that always upset me growing up was the fact we never had food. I believe that kids should never have to worry about utilities being cut off or having enough food to eat. I began to recognize a pattern with my mother: when she got food stamps; certain people would show up at our house. My mom would have new clothes, Incense would be burning, and we had lots of crap in the refrigerator. Sometimes my mother would give us one dollar in food stamps and tell us to go buy a twenty-five cent pack of gum. We would do this for about five times because they would give us back three quarters. She would then get the money and spend it for things like laundry, but most of the time it was to get in the club.

My brothers did not care—as long as there was food in the house. They were in heaven for the moment, but I knew within two weeks the beatings would be back. She would be frustrated because she spent all her money and sold all the food stamps. So, guess who the punching bag was? I see why my brothers left for days and moved in with their friends. I did not want to abandon my mother, so I kept trying anything to make her happy. But all my mother was looking for was the bottom of the bottle and nasty men that cared nothing about her.

Eventually my mother met a man who wanted her despite her flaws. I saw my mother happy for the first time in a while. She was like a little girl who just found love for the first time. Within months the two moved in together and within a year the fights started.

My stepdad had two sons and my mother had us younger two, my little brother and me. We were fourteen and twelve when we moved in with our stepdad. At first, I thought, "Finally we have a normal life. No more worrying about food, lights, or having running water. My stepdad saved us, and I thank God for that." But it didn't last long. My mom would accuse him of cheating and glasses would fly. If you disagreed with her you better watch your back, because something might be flying across the room. We barely had any plates in the house growing up because she would throw them in a minute if she thought you backed-talked her. I'm sure my stepdad cheated on my mother because he wanted out. He couldn't abandon her because he knew she was unable to take care of herself.

The fights continued and my mother started acting differently towards me. I was fifteen years old and my mother wanted to start walking to lose weight. On one day my stepdad joined us. I heard them fussing in the car before I got in. My stepdad said, "Are you serious? I would never touch our daughter!" I was shocked and I wanted to run. They didn't know I heard because I was just coming down the steps to the car. My mom looked up at me and smiled like nothing was wrong. My stepdad couldn't even move his head from looking crazily at my mother.

I sat in the back seat and was completely silent. What the hell did I just hear? Did he just... Did she just...? I was so confused.

We got to the park and my mother started down the trail. I followed her, still not talking. We did the whole two miles not saying one word to each other. Right before we got back to the car my mother said, "He probably thinks I've been questioning you this whole time." And that was it. She never even looked at me.

The following month I went to Elreno, Oklahoma. My biological father has family there and his sister would always call to check in on us because our dad never did. She would drive into the city to pick me up when her health would allow. She was extremely sick from time to time so, I would agree to clean her house and she would pay me. Her house was like an episode of Hoarders. She would buy and buy and buy things for no reason. Her parents owned the home, so she pretty much just did whatever she wanted with her money. One thing she never did was clean. It took me all weekend just to clean the kitchen and clear a space in the living room for her to sleep. I would sleep in my cousin's room and he would stay at his friend's house for the night.

On this one day, my cousin came in very drunk and was in his room trying to wake me up. "Hey Tiffany! Hey Tiff. Tifff." I kept my eyes closed tight. I thought he would just leave. Next thing I knew he was on top of me and my face was in the pillow. I was so scared, I was frozen stiff. My whole body locked up and I was completely dead inside. I wanted to run but I was so far away from home. Help me please, God is all I was thinking. I'm never leaving home again.

I remember the pillow being completely wet from my tears. He passed out beside me. The whole night I never moved.

In the morning his alarm went off and he jumped up. "Oh shit," he stated, "I got to go pick up my girlfriend. Get your things, I'll take you home." This wasn't anything new; he always took me home when I came here for the weekend. My aunt is usually too tired to make the drive back to my house. But this guy just went about his routine as if nothing just happened. I made my way to the car and tried to sit in the back seat.

"What are you doing?" my cousin said.

I said, "Your girlfriend is coming, right? She can sit in the front seat with you. I don't mind."

"No, no," he stated, "you in the front." And he just smiled. I sat with my hands in my lap until we got to his girlfriend's house. Ok, great, I thought, she will come around to the passenger side and I will get out and get in the back. Simple plan, Tiffany, you can do this. I started acting brave in my head, but the moment came, and his girlfriend came to my side. My cousin waved her to the back, and she didn't even look at me.

The ride home was so unconformable. He would rub my shoulders and tell stories of when we were younger to his girlfriend. I wanted to cry so bad, but I had to hold it together. I told myself I would never have to see these people again. I was running because I did not have the strength to face something like this, not on my own, and I had no one to help me.

We finally made it to my house, and he let me out at the curb. I ran into the house and my mother was drunk and fighting with my stepdad. I walked into my room and cried for about a week straight. I didn't even go to class. That's when I figured I could do pretty much whatever I wanted, and no one would care. So, I dropped out of high school, and just as I predicted my mother didn't even bat an eye. She told me, "I dropped out, you don't need to go." My mom got pregnant in high school and she later received her G.E.D. I really don't know why I left high school. I was passing all my classes, but something told me to not go back and I just listened to what was driving.

I was nineteen when I decided to move out of my mother's house, and what pushed me to move happened on my nineteenth birthday. My mom decided to throw this big barbecue. I remember her friends from work showing up, along with my brother and his friend, and I had invited a co-worker—an old Mexican lady named Juanita. We worked at the Air Force base together, but she had called earlier and said she was going to be late. Thank God for that, because the fight that happed was so embarrassing.

My brother was out on the back patio playing the music. I asked him for his CD case. My brother was talking with one of his friends when I asked, but he looked up and said, "Tiffany, don't look in my case." I did not listen and went to open it. I had always gone through his music, so I didn't understand the big deal.

Let's back up a few days prior. My boyfriend's CDs were stolen out of my room. I asked everyone in the house if they had seen these CDs. His name was written on them. Now, back to the party: as soon as I opened the case, the first CD had my boyfriend's name on it in black Sharpie. I looked up in slow motion and my brother's eyes were so big, but he had the nerve to be mad at me. I was so mad, but also confused. As I tried to analyse how I should be feeling, my brother was in my face. We screamed at each other so loudly. I then looked shocked, and that's when he knew he had me. I've noticed that throughout the years, depending on the situation, my family would miniplate me to the point I felt like everything was my fault and I ultimately apologize. My brother saw my face, and my face said I'm sorry for opening your CD case when you clearly told me no. You see, these people where my abusers, and I did obey him.

Before I knew it, my mother was in my face. She pulled me down the hall, saying how dare I mess up her party. She pushed me into my bedroom and began to punch me. My nose bled, as it did all the time. I hated her so bad. She told me to clean myself up and get back out there. I fell asleep instead and woke up to someone pounding at my door. It was my brother stating that my friend from work was there.

I cleaned myself up and went to see Juanita. She had brought her sister and daughter. Juanita was between fifty-five and sixty, four-foot-eleven. Her sister looked the same, but her daughter was about five-foot-nine with gorgeous black shiny hair. She was a Latina model. Her mother looked at her with the most love I had ever seen. Juanita loved her daughter, and her daughter loved her. Looking back, I see these ladies were there for a reason. I didn't know or understand why, but one thing Mrs. Juanita said to me was, "Tiffany, I don't know what happen to you, but you need to leave." I began to cry and told her what just took place. Her eyes filled with tears and she prayed with me right there. We talked a little more before they headed out. I never saw her again after that night.

A few months later I decided I was going to move out. I started working for the oil industry. I worked in the electrical assembly department. My department worked twelve-hour shifts and I was the only straight woman during the night with a whole lot of men. I worked with some nice-looking men. One evening at work I notice a new guy. This guy was in great shape, wearing a beanie, and his coveralls were sleeveless. "Did he just cut the sleeves off the company uniform?" I was instantly smitten. His name was Lambert, but everyone called him Ben; still, to this day I don't really understand why. He had a necklace made from shells or something. He had just moved back from California. For the next few weeks, we ate lunch together. We talked about everything—mainly his country life. He didn't treat me like a piece of meat, probably because he was raised in a home with his mother, grandmother, and his two sisters. I even think his aunt had lived with them at one point. He knew how to talk to women. I'd never had a man just talk to me and hang out with me without sex being involved.

One night I left work at two a.m. My throat was killing me, but I had no medication at home. I called Lambert because I knew he would be up. He was off that day but working nights you keep your same schedule. Lambert answered on the first ring. He stated he was up and said I should swing by because he had something for a sore throat. When I got to his apartment, he had a friend over playing video games. I noticed it was one of our co-workers. The co-worker smiled so big when he saw my face, as if he thought I was there for a booty call. All I could think was great there's going to be gossip at work tomorrow. Lambert gave me the meds and made sure I got home before they started making me feel sleepy. Leaving his apartment, I knew he was special. Lambert was with me from that day forward. He was at my place every day. The only reason we went to his place was for more clothes. My apartment was three minutes from our job, and we had the same hours, so it was perfect.

One morning Lambert went off to work a few hours early. I walked him to the door and gave him a kiss and told him I'd see him in a few. I locked the door and chilled out on the couch in his oversize t shirt. Moments later there's a knock at the door. I figured it was Lambert forgetting something, but when I opened the door I was surprised. It was a co-worker that I used to mess around with. Everyone at work knew Lambert and I were a couple. He pushed his way past me and I asked him what he wanted. He stated I knew exactly what he wanted. The bastard wanted sex. He had been watching, and when he saw Lambert drive off, he made his way to me. I figured his wife must be holding off from his lying, cheating ass. He grabbed me and turned me around. I felt him slide deep inside me. I hated every minute of it, but I didn't fight. I didn't see a point. The quicker it was over the quicker I could forget about it, or so I thought.

I chose not to tell Lambert about that evening for over nine years. I refused to think of that day. So, I made myself forget about it, and it was easy to forget because four weeks after that night Lambert and I were playing video games and drinking beer after work and for some reason I was unable to keep my beer down, though I didn't tell Lambert. The next morning, I went to the drugstore and purchased a pregnancy test. Sure enough, I was pregnant. I made an appointment as soon as possible. The earliest available OBGYN appointment was two weeks out.

By the time I got into the office and had the lab results back I was almost out of the first trimester. The morning sickness was supposed to go away after the first trimester, or so I thought. I was sick though out the whole pregnancy. The doctor didn't believe me until I went in for the second ultrasound. My fluid was so low they wouldn't let me leave the office. I was later sent home hooked up to an IV and with a nurse for the next few days. The only thing I was able to keep down was milk, apples, and chicken. From what I read, pregnancy wasn't supposed to be this hard, but I had no one to talk to, no one to compare this experience with. So, like I always do, I communicated with the doctor—but like always, I over communicated, and they just assumed I was overreacting. So, I begin to talk with God. I prayed for my baby to be special. And I asked God. I said, God showed me her skin and I began to focus on a beautiful baby girl with gorgeous skin, but he also showed me teaching her how to crawl. This did nothing but confuse me because the child I was teaching how to crawl was much older than a baby and why would you teach a child how to crawl? This later becomes clear what God was showing me.

I was thirty-four weeks when I delivered Torri via C-section. She was in distress and they had to go in and take her. Torri was in NICU for four weeks. She was so gorgeous. Her skin was two different complexions; she had red swirls all over her body. After about two months her red swirls became a smooth milk chocolate complexion, but the other light complexion was still there. This was my daughter's skin, a mixture of light and dark. She was a twist cone from an ice cream shop.

Torri's skin was not the only thing noticeable different. Her head size measured larger than it should, and she was behind according to the milestone charts. We went to every specialist, and the first one to shed some light to my daughter's condition was the genetics specialist. This specialist had only seen this condition one time before and he couldn't tell me anything about it—just she would probably live to the age of six. Just six years with my daughter was all they were giving me, and I didn't know how to take this information. I did research and stayed on top of her medication. No one was going to take my daughter away from me, not even God, and I was going to try everything in my power to save her. Or so I thought. Hypomelanosis Of Ito was my daughters' condition and the internet back in 2003 had little to no information on this disorder. From my understanding Ito was the doctor that discovered it and the swirls were Blaschko's Lines. These lines become apparent when a disease of the skin or mucosa manifest themselves according to these patterns. She had a "V" shape over the back, "S" shaped whirls over the chest and sides, and wavy shapes on the head. She had this swirling skin from head to toe and it would not fade or change over time, this was her. What's was the hardest part about raising a special needs child is the fact I never heard my daughter tell me she loved me. I didn't mind the many doctor appointments because I would do anything for her. Torri never was able to walk or talk but she loved music and I'm talking every type from country to rock; rap and I'm talking hard core was her thing. She loved an album called "Welcome to the Church "by a well-known rapper and this is how I got her to smile in school pictures. I remember the first time I had the guts to try this method. I first just had the music in her ears, but you could see the cords and I really wanted a good picture. So, I took out the CD and asked one of the teachers if I could put this in the computer. When Torri heard her song her eyes lite up like a Christmas tree. Everyone started laughing and then they heard the lyrics. I screamed "I'm a good mom don't judge me". I was so ashamed of what I was doing just to get her to smile. Everyone continued to laugh, and one lady told me to relax Torri's happy and that's all that matters right now.

In the following years my relationship with Lambert became rocky. My mother lived with us on and off. We would move in with her to help her with the bill because she just couldn't handle living on her own. We had a good routine going with Torri, and six years later we had another little girl. I never thought about the sixth year as the final year for Torri. We had surgery to implant a device to help combat the seizures. The V.N.S (Vagus Nerve Stimulator) was implanted into my daughter's chest at Cooks Children Hospital in Fort Worth Texas. This hospital was top of the line, and the epilepsy section of the hospital was everything a child with seizures needed. The children in this portion of the hospital had to have an EGG attached to their head for five days or longer so the doctors could catch all the seizure activity. Most of the time the children had to be in the bed, but at this hospital they were able to move about and even go to different playrooms on the ward. After the device was implanted, Torri's seizures were under control for about a year. Pregnant with our third child, Lambert and I decided to move to his hometown of Hominy, Oklahoma.

We lived in Hominy, Oklahoma, for four years. This wasn't easy country living. Hominy was a tiny town in the middle of nowhere. This was Osage County and most of the land was Native American territory. Hominy had one stop light, two gas stations, a pizza parlour, and a bank. It was right next to the town Pawhuska where the Drumming Lady from the Food Network Channel lived. However, "country" was an understatement. I had no clue what I signed up for, but I had just married this man and we had three kids now. I told God I was going to try and make this marriage work.

Lambert's whole family lived in Hominy and I was excited to get to know his sisters. For years I thought how it would be to have a sister and now I had four. Two of his sisters lived in town and I would invite them over for dinner all the time. I slowly started noticing that his sisters didn't care for me. They would state I was "acting white." I've heard this all my life. These women were those types of people. From that moment I knew I was never going to be able to get along with most of the people in this town. Most of the people there never left and refused to. The only joy in their lives was laughing at others and gossiping. Lambert was like a local legend because of all his records he set in high school. Some of the women had always dreamed of dating the high school jock, and nothing stopped them from trying; even the wedding ring on his finger couldn't keep these women away.

I will never forget the day of April 24th, 2014. Triston our other daughter who was just 6yrs old at the time, had a school activity we all were attending, but my mother was going to stay back with Torri because she wasn't feeling well. We were at the school for almost an hour and my mother called saying Torri had been having seizures for about five minutes now and it was unbelievably bad. We rushed home and the ambulance was there. Torri was rushed to the closest hospital, which was in the next town. We stayed there until they had her stable enough to get her to Children's hospital in Tulsa, Oklahoma. Torri went into a coma for three months and that's when I found out my husband was cheating on me with one of the moms that helped on Triston's T-ball team.

I wanted nothing more than to give up at that moment, but I couldn't because my daughter needed me. All my kids needed me. So, I turned to God and asked for strength, and on Mother's Day Torri opened her eyes. She was not awake, and they had to keep her in a coma because of all the seizure activity, but this was the sign I needed to hang in there. I pushed everything aside and became a great, devoted wife. I told myself, "I will win my husband back and Torri will come home." I set out a plan to confront my so-called friend, but God stopped me and I never saw her again.

Three months later Torri came home from the hospital and I waited until she was healthy enough to make the move back to Oklahoma City. Hominy was not the place for my family to live. Most of the people were racist, or too afraid to stand up and become who God truly intended them to be. I did have some good times. There were great antique shops, and the Native American art was amazing.

The move was quite easy. My plan was to sell everything except what we absolutely needed, and we would just buy things as we got a little money. The whole town knew about Lambert's affair and I could feel all the whispers through town. My mother would just roll her eyes from time to time. I always felt her judging me. My mother's time in Hominy was extremely hard on me as well. I started seeing more and more of the episodes (which later became known as seizures). These episodes were her calling me a different name and would lick her lips several times and stirring off into space. I would try and get her attention by asking her question, but she would not respond, or she would act like she was talking but she wouldn't make a sound. She never remembered these events, and that made things more difficult. She began to accuse me of lying and we would fight all the time. Nevertheless, I still took care of her because I knew she was sick. I just did not know how bad it was.

Back in Oklahoma City was where I needed to be. Torri had an amazing team of doctors and she was going to therapy every week.

I started thinking about the long-term care for Torri and how hard it would be for me to take care of her. We had a nurse come out, but I had to let her go because she was doing weird stuff and wouldn't let me in the room one time when she was changing my daughter.

I thought maybe I could have her in a facility a few days a week if I worked there. So, I applied for the nursing program and got accepted. I was going to become a nurse and work wherever Torri was. On my fourth day in the program I was on the highway, almost to class, when I got a phone call from Lambert my husband at the time.

"Tiffany hurry and get home," Lambert said. "Torri had a seizure and she's not breathing." At that moment God told me to talk to her as if she was right beside me, so I did. I said, "Torri, I love you with all my heart. You were everything I asked God for and more. I don't want you to come to me. Don't come visit me. I want you to live. Live a happy, full life with no pain. I loved being your mother and for 13 years I got to see your beautiful face every day. I got these two down here. Go be free, my love. I will miss you like crazy. I love you".

At home I ran into the room and the paramedic was pushing on Torri's chest. I ran to find my other kids and I looked at my mom and I said, "She's gone, Mom," and just started crying. My mom fell out on the floor. I couldn't even be sad because my mom was acting, and I was too through with her, so I turned my attention to Triston and Lawrence. I hugged them so tight and cleaned their faces. I told them to stay with Grandma and help her. That would keep them busy and their minds off the event taking place in the other room.

They continued CPR on the ride to the hospital. Lambert rode with them and my neighbour drove me. They tried for over an hour and the doctor finally walked over to me and said, "Mrs. Johnson, we have given her—"

I stopped her and said, "I understand everything that your team has tried to do for my daughter. Go ahead and call it."

She looked so shocked. She grabbed my hand and we walked in the room. There were about seven doctors in there and one was on top of the table. I walked in the room and the doctor stated, "Mom is here, and she said we can call it." Everyone looked at me and dropped their heads. I heard someone say the time, but all I could do was just look at Torri. I told myself she was just tired. The doctors slowly left the room, and my husband and brother came in. I looked up at them and said, "She's just tired." My brother tried to hug her, but he was so upset because she was still hooked up to everything. All I could do was say over and over that she was just tired. She was just tired. She was just tired. I became louder and louder. I didn't even know I was screaming. Everyone left and I was alone, crying, screaming. A nurse had to come and shut the door at one point. I told her one last time I loved her, and she could rest. I left that hospital without my daughter, my greatest fear come true.

Leaving the hospital without Torri was so confusing. I remember feeling like I was forgetting something. I've left that hospital several times without Torri. Usually, it was to get clothes because we were admitted from one of the many trips to the ER. But this time was different. I knew I wasn't coming back for her and this pain was killing me.

The drive home was noticeably quiet. Lambert was looking at peace and this made me even more confused. When we pulled up to our home our neighbours came over and prayed with us in our front yard. They were a young couple with 2 children of their own. I remember one morning I woke up to them building a ramp for or front steps. They seen me struggle time and time again when I would take Torri out the house. I hope they know how much we appreciated that ramp. Walking in the house Lambert still had this peaceful look on his face and I finally asked him "are you ok" He looked over at me and said, "I seen them take her". "Lambert what are you talking about". I thought he might be losing his mind. I mean we just lost our daughter this could be shock. Lambert begin to tell me that Torri had a seizure, but he used the magnet and it had stopped. He then notices she needed her diaper changed and he said as soon as he unfastens the tabs on the diaper, she stopped breathing and time stopped. He stated everything was frozen. He then explained, two what he believed to be angels flew through the window and took her. I knew what he had just told me was true because the week before I prayed to God and I told him please send the best angels for my baby girl I cannot have her traveling alone. I also told Torri that I was stronger now and she did not have to stay for here for me. If I knew that was going to be my last week with her, I would have hugged her longer.

After Torri's death everything that was put on the back burner moved forward. Lambert and I were over. The fact that he was messing around with my best friend when our daughter was in the hospital fighting for her life needed to be on the front burner and handled and I felt two could play that game. I started to let loose. I didn't want to think about not having Torri in my life, I wanted nothing more than to forget everything. I begin fixing my hair and meeting up with guys. Some were old friends, others complete strangers.

But when I reconnected with one old friend, I completely stopped with the random ones and he became my world. Whatever this Polynesian god told me to do I did. All I wanted to do was to make him happy, and to make him happy I did anything he asked. I needed structure, so I put people in charge of me because I wanted to belong to someone or something. My family never felt like my family. I grew up doing whatever I chose because my mom was working some crap-hole job or off with another boyfriend. So, I set the Polynesian god in charge and every moment became him.

I was in love with him, or so I thought. He was born in Hawaii and I first met him when I was fourteen through his sisters. They both knew of my relationship with their brother. They never spoke a word of it to any other family members. He was married at the time, but I did not care. Now after all these years he was married again, and once again I did not care. He lived in Colorado and he would have me drive for eight hours to spend the weekends locked in a hotel room with him. I just wanted to be wanted. God gave me exactly what I asked for, which was not much, because I did not think much of myself. I hated who I was.

One morning I heard him calling into work. The excuse was that he had to take his wife to dialysis. His wife was dealing with severe health issues and she did not have long to live if she didn't receive a kidney. I always asked how she was doing. Part of it was because I was really concerned. Being a mother to a special needs child, I knew all about the countless doctor appointments. But the other part of me was thinking, maybe her spot will become available. I was in complete love and he knew exactly what to say for me to go crazy. All he had to do was tell me I was the one that got away and how much he was in love with me. I believed every word. He liked to "show me" how much he missed me by sending me videos of him pleasuring himself. I told him it turned me on, but it never did. I wanted him to believe that I was made for his sick twisted mind, and if that meant losing who I was then so be it. I just wanted to feel wanted.

He told me I needed to move to Colorado. He was going to help me get an apartment, but I just couldn't take the kids away from their dad for this part time man. I knew deep down he was never going to leave his wife, but I was holding on. Holding on to false hopes and dreams. If this man was cheating on his dying wife, what made me so special? I wanted to believe someone thought I was good enough. I knew he wasn't the man for me, so I stopped talking with him. I blocked him on everything and told his sisters to say they no longer talk to me.

About 6 months after Torri passed away, I began working for a pain management doctor. I was the phlebotomists, and I had my own little lab. The doctor was about 65 and he had never been married or had any children. He took a shin to me and we started going to lunch together along with the other doctors. It was going great or so I thought. After about a year the doctor was having money issues and he enlisted the help of a management firm. They came in talking about how much he could be making but a lot of changes needed to be made. I was replaced in my lab by one of there lab people. He would not let them fire me, so they made me become his personal assistant which doc loved. I had to pay his bills, handle his dry cleaning, and take him shopping, and on the weekends as well. I even assisted this man in surgeries. But one of the things I enjoyed most was taking care of his dogs. He had some of the best dogs I've had ever seen. They were golden retrievers. I couldn't think of owning a dog with everything I was going through so to be able to experience this type of selfless love was what I needed at that moment. His dogs not only brought joy to my life but to my children as well. Being doc personal assistant had its benefits at times. I got to drive his nice sports car and house sit for the week. His house was on the lake and the whole back wall was glass. The kids loved staying the night at doc's house and so did I. It was an escape from reality. Escaping reality would make me happy for the moment but I did not want to be happy for the moment anymore. I wanted to be happy in real life.

So, one night I said, "Dear heavenly Father, I thank you for allowing me to see the true beauty in things. I ask for whatever I am meant to do; please show me. I will not fight it anymore. I am ready… I have been running long enough. Just show me one sign." At about eleven o'clock that night, my Fitbit dinged. I looked up at God and said, "Are You kidding me?" It was a message from Jason. I remember earlier that day I was trying to be more active on my

Fitbit. So, I started friending people on Fitbit and Jason a guy all the way in Washington DC sent me a message saying, "Thanks for the add." I was confused, but I replied, "No problem." He continued the conversation with talks about steps and goals with the Fitbit and how we both loved the fitness device. We were both in the group that needed to lose 50lbs or more. I was definitely more. My weight had got up round the 300 mark. And Jason was around 400lbs. The next day he texted me again through the app. We talked about football. He thought I was a Dallas fan. "Sorry Sir I am not," I told him. We only texted through the Fitbit app for about a week before I gave him my number. The following morning, I received a text asking how many steps I had. I smiled so big. I was finally talking with him through my actual phone instead of the app.

We texted for another two weeks. What was strange was he never tried to call, though text was fine with me because I was still married, not to mention still sleeping in the same bed as my husband. Torri had been gone for two years now, and the kids' dad and I were not going to make it. But he loved his kids and he had time for them where I had none. I finally asked him to call me. He asked if I was sure. Why wouldn't I be sure? We've been texting for a while why wont this man try to call me. That very moment my phone rung and it was a DC number. I was so excited it him I thought. I asked, "Hello, Jason"? "Yes" he said, "How are you?" I'm good I stated. Something was wrong. He doesn't sound like I was expecting. Oh, I wonder if he's deaf. Jason had a very strange speech impediment. I had the hardest time understanding him. But I could stop talking to him for this reason. We continued talking everyday and it slowly started getting easier to understand his language. I was to the point I was fluent in Jason's language.

Jason was ready to take our relationship to the next level and so was I, but for that to happen Lambert needed to know the truth. One night I sat down with Lambert and we talked about the relationship and where he thought it was going. We both wanted out, but we didn't know how to go about doing so. I told him I would move to the other bedroom. The kids could share a room and we could both save money. In a year's time we could go our separate ways. He looked confused, but he agreed. It had some bumps, but Lambert and I couldn't be happier with the decision.

I couldn't wait to tell Jason. Jason started right away planning our future. He told me he had been waiting for this moment for so long. He lived with his mom, but he made more than enough to provide. He started looking at homes. I was on FaceTime while he was viewing them. His smile was contagious. We stayed on the phone all day talking about what we needed to buy and what sports the kids would play. We planned out our future that year, writing everything down we needed to accomplish, and we did just that. On April 30th, 2018, we signed on our first home and everything was going amazing. I thought nothing could come between Jason and our love, but boy was I wrong.

Moving to Maryland from Oklahoma was a culture shock to say the least. I've never seen so many black people in one place and it was nothing like it was portrayed on TV. I was a little stand-offish so I took a job at a doctor office I thought would suit me.

The office was primary care which was a little different from pain management. We had a few pain managements cases but nothing I was used to. One of the women there called herself the Nazi nurse. She was 5'9 and about 180lbs. She had short spiked red hair. She was retired navy and she thought she was the best thing since sliced bread. She had a part time job with the police department. She was the person the police would call when there was a dead body on the scene. She loved pizza so for her birthday I got her a gift card to her favorite pizza restaurant. After her birthday was the month of February which is black history month. The nurse had made a comment stating why do we give them a whole month. She seen that I had overheard the conversation and she left the brake room. This woman never cared for me and I had seen why. She was talking to the doctor and the other staff. There was only 5 of us working in this office and I was the only black person there. I felt uncomfortable to say the least. The nurse continued to belittle me and on April 17, it happens, this crazy woman had put her hands on me. I was in a room with a patient going over her history as you do with new patients. I notice a mistake and was about to ask the patient a question, but the doctor walked in so I left to give them time to talk. I walked out into the lab and was finishing up what I could and I figured I would return when the doctor came out. Speeding down the hall was the nurse full of rage. She threw the patients history paperwork at me. "Did you see what year she put for her last pep? "Yes", I said. "She couldn't have meant to put a date that hasn't came yet." I'll ask her when the doctor leaves. The nurse grabs the paper out of my hands and walks in the room where the doctor and the new patient was. "When was your last pep she yells?" "2018" the patient states. The nurse walks back over to me and states 2018. I replied "yeah I heard you. I think the whole office heard you." I pick up my laptop and head down the hall to grab another patient. The nurse steps in front of me and stated I needed to watch myself. I try squeezing by her, but I was not getting through. I told her I needed to go room patients and she needed to move. She began to push her chest up against me and raised her hands up to knock my laptop up against my chain. She was doing this a few times and then she grabs my arm and pulls me into the front office. She stated she was going to have me fired. When we got to the front office I was upset because no one was there. Great, I needed someone to see what was happening. I put my laptop down on a chair and turned around to leave but she grabs me and pushes me against the wall. My head hit the wall and I knew I needed to do something, so I pushed her. I didn't just push her I mean I really pushed her. All I know is I watched her fly across the room and her feet went up in the air and the plant stand flew across the desk and I ran down the hall to the doctor's office and locked myself inside. A few moments later the receptionist comes down the hall screaming the nurse is down. The office manager came in and asked me what happened. I told her everything and I left that day and never returned. I went to press charges against her, but she had connection with the police, and I lost the case. The doctor office let her resign so she could continue nursing. I had told my family about the attack and of course I was made the butt of many jokes. My mother wanted to help, and she had convinced me to let her move in with me. My mother would call me and complain that she was not getting her blood pressure medication, and my brothers would not take her to the doctor. So, like always I was there for my mother in a blink of an eye.

Chapter 2

MOM IN MARYLAND

I always felt bad for my mom when she was living with my brothers. One brother had her sleeping on the floor. One even used her as a housekeeper and a nanny for his foster kids. I told him not to leave them alone with her because of the seizures, but not only did he continue to leave the foster kids with my mother, but he bought her a car. Which she wrecked because she was having a seizure. I couldn't get my brothers to listen to me for nothing.

When my mom moved in, I told her that she could have the master bedroom upstairs, closer to Triston and Lawrence. I wanted her to have a close relationship with her grandchildren because my mother and I weren't that close. I took her to get her nails done and her hair braided, and the most important part was Mom got insurance. The very first thing I did was get my mother health insurance because I knew she was having seizures, but I needed tests and a neurologist. I made myself a checklist because I still had a family at home, and I didn't want to forget any appointments. I needed to make Mom an appointment with her regular doctor (PCP), and from there the doctor would give us a referral for the specialist (the neurologist). Once we had that appointment and the neurologist saw the videos of all her what I believed to be seizures, he put a rush on the EEG (electroencephalogram) and Mom was giving medication to start once the EEG was complete. The morning of the EEG was August 13, 2019. And the weather was cloudy and sticky. It had been raining early that morning so the roads were still wet.

As I got off the highway, I could see the hospital straight in front of me. "Look, Mom, I found it." Mom looked over at me and smiled. I looked past her and saw something terrifying. She must have seen my face when I looked back at her, because my face made her whip her head back around so fast. I could do nothing but brace myself for impact. A Ford 350 electrical company truck hit us on my mother's side.

My mother was screaming in pain. I was fine or so I thought; my adrenaline was kicked in and I just needed help. I went to talk with the truck driver, but he jumped out and ran behind a tree and left his partner in the truck. Weird, I thought, but I went back to my mom. She was grabbing her chest and screaming. She had no visual cuts or anything of that nature. Cops came and the driver of the truck was back. We got checked out at the hospital and I went back to reschedule the EEG. On top of everything I was trying to do for my mom, now had to add more doctor appointments and physical therapy. I had a family of my own and she wasn't understanding. I would ask my mom to learn the metro. "We could learn together," I stated. "I'll think about it" was always the answer. Every time Mom had a seizure; I would let my brothers know. I thought they would want to keep up with their own mother's health. I was the only one who picked up on her patterns. After Mom's seizures she would be very tired and usually fall asleep. When she woke up she was angry, but not just angry—it was rage from something. Maybe a PTSD moment. One time Jason and I were in the living room and my mom came and stood in the hallway up against the wall and said, "I know you motherf*ckers been talking about me." Jason and I were completely dumbfounded. We got up and went downstairs and just sat in silence. We were so puzzled. Another time I was taking Mom to the store and my son was in the back seat. My mother's face started to twitch. Ok, I thought, this is a different type of seizure—lets go straight to the ER. I was talking to Mom, but she wasn't responding. This went on for about two minutes. When she finally came back, she was very calm and sweet.

"MOM," I said, "I'm taking you to the hospital."

"OK," she replied, still very calm.

"Do you know your name?"

She just said, "OK." When we pulled up at the hospital is when all hell broke loose. Mom looks me up and down and says, "Where are we?"

"Mom, you had a seizure. I told you I was taking you to the hospital."

"Hell no!" she said. "Take me home now."

"But Mom, you had a seizure, and it was different from the others. I went you to get checked out. Maybe they can do something, and we need documentation for disability."

"Fuck you! This has all been a scam!"

"What are you talking about?" I asked.

"You and Jason just want my money!"

I laughed a little bit because my mom couldn't be serious. This woman had no money, nothing, and now she was claiming I was trying to get her locked up to take her money. After I called one of my brothers and they told her to get out of the car, we finally went in. I recorded the seizure. I always recorded because I don't think I can give enough detail. Doctors usually want to know which side was moving so they can determine which part of the brain the seizure is coming from. My mom's seizures were coming from both sides. It's like everything was involved, but not to the point she was kicking about on the floor. After the doctors saw the video, they wanted to confirm they were seizures, but because we were in the ER they couldn't without proper tests, like an EEG. That was fine with me, if I got this ER visit documented maybe it could helped get my mother's disability.

The following month we got the EEG done. I informed my brother of what the doctor said. Mom was in fact having seizures and she must not drive. She had been on a low dose of medication called Keppra, but her neurologist wanted to increase the dosages. My daughter Torri was on this medication and I knew all too well of its side effects. Torri would take our hands and scream in our face. She would try and bite us, which was so odd because she had never done that in the past. Once I read the side effects it made sense. One of the side effects was anger. I kept my brothers in the loop, but they never replied much. I had a text group with all the boys and two of their wives. I wanted everyone to be involved in our mother's care. I also had one setup to include Mom so she could talk with everyone. I just wanted everyone to be this big happy family, but that was never going to happen. Mom was still unhappy. She would state things like "I don't even know why I'm alive," but mom always had her Bible in her hands.

At Thanksgiving 2019, my oldest brother came to visit. This was going to cheer mom up for sure. My brother was upstairs one evening and I heard him screaming my name. "Tiffany, come here! Something is wrong with Mom."

Mom had taken her cup of water and poured it on her lap. My brother was so confused. I told him those are her seizures. I reminded him I had sent him and the other brothers videos and messages explaining her seizures in the group chat. I rolled my eyes at him because they never listen to me. The following day Mom and I went to the store to start early Christmas shopping. In the car we discussed which wrapping paper the kids would have. We decided that one would have snowmen and the other would get the candy canes. We got upstairs and she wanted to start wrapping right away. I got her all the supplies she needed, and my doorbell rang. It was my neighbour from around the corner. My mother became angry. I saw my mother's face become upset. She didn't like me having company in my own home. One time she even slammed the door in one of my friends' faces.

Seeing she was getting upset, I took my neighbour outside to see what was going on. She just wanted to gossip about the school our daughters attended. I was outside for about ten minutes, and when I got back in the house my mother had wrapped all the gifts in the same wrapping paper.

"Mom, do you know which gift is whose?" I asked.

She looked at me as if I were crazy. She said, "Yes, I wrapped Triston's first and then Lawrence's next."

"OK, that's great, but they had the same shaped boxes. Do you know which one is who so I can put their names on it?" She looked at me crazy again. "Mom," I said, "what happened to them having different wrapping paper?"

She said, "If you don't like it you can do it yourself."

At that point, my brother woke up from the chair and asked what was going on. My mom said, "Tiffany don't like the way I'm wrapping the presents."

My brother got upset and said, "Tiffany, wrap the shit yourself if you don't like it."

"No, that's not it," I said. "Mom and I agreed on wrapping the gifts in different paper. I just wanted to know if she knew what name I needed to write." My brother kept arguing with me and I finally started screaming. "IT'S NOT THAT I DON'T THINK SHE DID A GOOD JOB WRAPPING. I'M JUST TRYING TO FIGURE OUT WHAT NAME TO WRITE." Then they focused on my screaming and I just went downstairs to cool down. Jason was right by my side. My brother came downstairs and stood in front of me with his arms folded and stated he knew how to handle people like me because he was a cop. Now this is the same man that was fighting at my daughter's funeral so I could only image what he was going to do to me, but I told him he had to leave my house and that was the last time my brother was at my home. Jason was not happy about the way my family treated me, but I told him several times about how they act.

The next few months the house became dark, and the energy surrounding everyone had changed. No one was happy in our home. My daughter was getting bullied at school. I started questioning my decision about moving to Maryland and thought maybe I needed to move back to Oklahoma. I told my mother and she said all I had to do was say the word and she could make a phone call. She was ready in a moment's notice, but her seizures were not getting better. And I loved Jason so much, but I just didn't understand why we were fighting so much.

Triston knew her grandmother had seizures and was able to help because I always explained what was happening with Torri. Triston and I had a plan just in case she saw Mom have one and I wasn't around. She'd seen me jump into action a few times, and I always wondered how she was feeling. Triston is very sympathetic to everyone's feelings, to the point that when she was being bullied at school, she would make excuses for their behaviour and tell me things like, "He's probably getting hit by his dad or brothers, that's why he spit on me." Being a Mom, I was furious not at my daughter but myself. This is my behaviour. I allow people to walk all over me because their lives and whatever it was they were going through was more important than what I was going through. I didn't even allow myself to mourn the loss of my daughter because I was too worried about everyone else during that time. I had to teach my daughter to stand up for herself. But how could I teach my daughter to stand up for herself when I couldn't lead by example? My mom and Triston's relationship was close, or so I thought. Triston just felt bad for her grandmother and just wanted to make her happy. I told her that she was only twelve, and it was not her job to make her happy. I wish someone would have told me that when I was younger.

One morning I received the phone call from the school counsellor about my son Lawrence, I was confused. At home he was your typical boy, in his room playing video games or outside playing football. I was not ready for what she told me. The counsellor stated my son had been crying and telling her he was thinking of killing himself. Lawrence wouldn't state why, just that he was unhappy.

I called one of my other brothers because they deal with these types of situations and asked what I should do. He said I should take him to the hospital and have them do an evaluation. Once they told Lawrence they had to draw blood, Lawrence said he was fine and didn't want to be there. The doctor told us we could leave and that I should encourage him to share his feelings, so I did. Lawrence's attitude changed and he seemed to be better, but something was not right. So, I made it a point to pay extra attention to him. We went on mom and son dates and just hung out more, which he loved. Maybe that's all he needed. He had been through a lot for his age. He was just nine years old and he had seen his oldest sister die, his parents' divorce, a huge move 1200 miles away from his father, and now his grandmother was there having seizures and his mother's time is everywhere else. Yes, my son needed time with his mom so I could reassure him everything was going to be OK.

God was showing me that I needed to get my house in order, and the next step was moving back upstairs. So, I asked my mom to move downstairs because Jason and I wanted to get closer to the kids and being downstairs we felt a disconnect from them. Mom said no at first, but I told her it would feel like her own apartment. She had a bedroom, bathroom, and a living area. Mom was not happy, and she started acting like Jason was trying something with Triston. It got to the point that Jason said he was getting uncomfortable with the way she treated him. Jason told me he understood that Triston is her granddaughter, and maybe Mom was just being cautious. But Jason also let me know that if we ever had kids, she would not be treating him like he was a paedophile. God said, "Put all your trust in me" and that's what I did. On Easter 2020 I let go and I let God.

It was Easter Sunday of all days. We were all getting ready for Easter dinner and we had a feast going. Mom was making the meatloaf and I was on macaroni and cheese duty. I had been trying out a new recipe and I still didn't have it down.

While we cooked, something told me to look at Mom, and when I did, she was licking her fingers. I immediately told Triston to get my phone and start recording. The video shows me grabbing my mother's hands out of her mouth and turning her around to wash her hands and face. My mother was eating raw meatloaf mix with raw meat, eggs, and all the veggies. I got her cleaned up and walked her down the hall to have a seat while I processed what just happened. I sent the video to my brothers and I sent an email to her neurologist with the recording as well.

My oldest brother texted our mother and ask her, "What's going on? Tiffy said you tripping." Why did he do that? Now she was going to be in a rage because she thought I was talking behind her back—and guess who she was going to attack? I don't know why, but it's always about betrayal after a seizure. My mom jumped up and came at me screaming. "Don't be telling my boys about me! It isn't none of their got damn business." I never understood why she didn't want them to know—why I was the one that had to handle everything without help. She became so outraged. She told my bother that she wanted to move, and that I was trying to lock her downstairs. My mom kept screaming and calling me all kinds of names. My oldest brother told her to call the police on us and she did.

That's when I decided I was done with this. She had the cops at my door. I told Jason, "We pay for that cell phone, and I'm taking it away." If I had to treat her like a child, then so be it. I went into the room, grabbed the phone from my mother's hands, and told her she was not going to treat me like this anymore. No one cared for her the way I did, and I couldn't help her anymore. I did everything I could do. God said it was time for me to start focusing on my family. God told me that to break this generational curse I needed to remove myself from the whole family tree and start fresh.

The following day my mother had a plane ticket to Texas. But I wanted to disobey God one more time and try to get my mom to stay. I didn't believe I had to let my mother go. Even when it was so clear she didn't want to be here. Before my mom walked out the door, I told her, "Mom, you don't have to go. We can work this out." I have never hugged my mom. I didn't talk in school until the 3rd grade. So, I also asked my mom for a hug just to show her I can do this and I cared for her.

She didn't even look back at me. All I heard her say under her breath was, "Fuck you bitch," and that was all I needed to hear to know I made the right choice in letting her go. I couldn't believe this was my family I was fighting to keep in my life. When Jason got back from taking Mom to the airport, we just stared at each other and I said, "I told you my family was crazy." We laughed and just went back to bed.

Over the next few weeks, we received some crazy messages from my mother. She stated that Jason was keeping me from my family and abusing the kids. My mother even called my ex-husband and his mother to tell then to check on the kids. After receiving the news, that she was calling my ex-mother-in-law, I called my brother and asked him what was going on. He said they were just concerned about the kids.

At this point I was completely puzzled. Jason just told me to leave it alone and that she would calm down eventually. Oh, that was the complete opposite of the truth. My mom started sending Jason messages stating he was going to answer to God for keeping her daughter away from her and that she was going to take us to court. My mother was truly an emotional wreck, and I was over 1200 miles away. I couldn't focus on her anymore. I was worried about my mother, but God showed me it wasn't my responsibility to make her happy. I was in control of my life, not hers.

I began to exercise and got back to my Fitbit. I started to talk with my kids more. I found out just how much Triston liked painting, and realized she wanted to give up sports to focus more on her art. For a twelve-year-old to tell her parents this was serious. She knew how much we loved seeing her perform in track. But our relationship had become so much better since my mother left, and

God knew what He was doing, so I worked out a deal with Triston. "You can focus on your art," we told her, "but you still must eat in a healthy manner and you still must run four days a week." She was more than excited to accept the offer.

Lawrence finally told me what had made him think about suicide. It was my mother. She would talk down to him when I wasn't around. I knew she thought Lawrence was mischievous, but I never knew what she would say to him until he told me. After hearing the names, I had no doubt she said those things because those were the names she called me. I wasn't close to him when my mother was around, and back when Torri was alive, I never had time for Triston or Lawrence because I was taking care of Torri. Their dad or my mother had them, and I could only imagine how my son felt.

A few months after my mother left everything just seemed brighter. I looked around and everyone had a glow about them. My son busted out one evening and said, "The dark cloud is finally gone, huh Mom?" I looked over at him and said, "It sure is."

The next few months were just about getting the house in order. It was about reclaiming my home. I started to enjoy making over the living room, so we decided to create a space for the kids in the spare bedroom. "How about a game room?" I asked Jason. Sure enough, he was on board. Everything came out amazing—even Triston got creative and painted video game characters on the chalkboard wall. We then travelled to Colorado for a few weeks. Jason was working, and I got to spend more time with the kids.

I found myself so inspired by them. At just ten and twelve they had this faith in them that I couldn't believe. I asked them where this belief in God came from and why they felt the way they did. Triston told me that she could feel how others felt and the pain that some people go through is unbearable, but if you put your trust in God then things aren't as bad as we thought, and before you know it the pain is over. I remember years ago when Triston was a toddler, I would say positive things to her, but mostly I was saying them to myself. I was finally seeing the puzzle coming together, and it was the most beautiful picture I could ever imagine. By moving to Maryland God showed me I was never close with my family because I was never meant to stay with my family. To break generational curses, you sometimes—not all the time, but sometimes—have to remove yourself from the family tree, plant new roots, and start new. One piece of the puzzle God showed me was why He gave me a child like Torri with special needs. My mother beat the crap out of me, and as I thought this was normal behaviour, I might have done the same thing to Torri. Since she was born with HI/HA syndrome, I could never touch my baby girl in that manner. Thank You, God.

The wedding date was set. We knew we were going to have it downstairs and invite maybe twenty people. The only thing is I had no family coming whatsoever. Even if we were on speaking terms, I would not want them at my wedding. This meant that Jason could invite more of his family since we had limited space.

One evening I received a message. It was a group chat I was in with some old friends I reconnected with from nursing school. One of the girls sent a joke. Everyone laughed and all shared updates on each other's lives. I told everyone I was getting married and they were so supportive. I thought they were genuinely happy for me. I told them if they wanted to come, they could stay at my home with me and my family. Never in a million years did I think they would take me up on the offer, but sure enough they did. All four said they were down for the wedding party. Crap! In all honesty I did not remember any of them! From what I remember of the nursing program I was in, I left three months before graduation. It was clinicals and all I could think about was Torri laying in those hospital beds. As I try and recall these ladies to Jason, I realized I was having a hard time placing them in my life back then. I hung out with Becky from time to time; Rose came to Lawrence's birthday party along with Becky. I bumped into Tracy at the gym years ago. Other than that, we'd only seen each other's posts on social media. I was at a complete loss as into why they wanted to come and see me, but God told me that they needed to be here. I was completely trusting God at this point and it felt great. I had no worries or fears. Well, maybe some little fears, but Jason always reassured me everything was going to work out. I told myself to push through because we had about two months to get things together. Jason and I transformed the downstairs completely. The walls were Portuguese dawn, and the border was frosted ivory. I had flower draping everywhere and Jason even built the altar. Everything was perfect.

Chapter 3

Pick-Up Day

Now, you would think with four girls they would just take an Uber from the airport. I sent a message asking if they needed my address. They pretty much said I better not leave them stranded at the airport. Great. I let people push me around my whole life. It was time for me to start standing up for myself. So, I guess they are not getting an Uber.

I told Jason and he was so upset with me. "I'm putting these girls up in my home during our wedding, and now we have to drive to pick them up from the airport, Tiffany," Jason said. "Fine, let's go get them from Reagan National."

"Uh, so... that's not where they are." I was so scared to tell Jason this next part, but I had to. "Jason, see, everyone just assumes because we live in Maryland that Baltimore is the closest airport."

"What?" he screamed. "Now I'm driving damn near three hours in total because they don't know how to book the correct airport? And they can't even divide the cost for a Uber."

I'm a bunch of talk, but I just learn and move on. I told myself it's not a big deal and guess what—it wasn't. I enjoyed the drive to the airport because I had time to talk with God. I cried and told him that I trusted Him to the fullest and I was ready to rock and roll. I got to the airport a little late and they were all sitting on a bench, but Teah was in a wheelchair. I didn't see this coming! I have stairs, I was thinking to myself. Everyone was quiet because my face was in shock, I guess. After a few seconds Teah jumped up and screamed, "I got ya!" My heart hit the ground so hard I almost passed out.

We got to the house and I showed them their rooms. They slept two to a room, but during the night Becky would wander out to the couch because Tracy sounded like a freight train with her snoring.

The next day was the big day. I had no time to be nervous; I was putting on a wedding and it was time to rock and roll. That morning I went to get my nails done while Jason got things together downstairs with the last-minute deliveries. We still hadn't seen each other, and it was everyone's job in the house to make sure of this. I got back and jumped in the kitchen. I was making huge pans of baked ziti and alfredo with shrimp and chicken, as well as salad and garlic bread. We also had cocktail hour before and after the ceremony.

That morning I received a phone call from Jason. He told me how excited he was and how we finally did it. He then told me to look under the TV in our room. It was an envelope. He hung up and I read it. It was a letter from Jason telling me not to worry. That no matter what, he had me. I cried but I shook it off. Today I was getting married and I had no time for those emotions.

Next step was the kids. This whole time my two were hanging in like champions. Triston's opinion meant a lot to me. Sure, my daughter was just thirteen, but her personality was of a sixty-year-old at times. She was wise beyond her years—an old soul, if you will. I knew I needed her to see me change who I was for her to make changes in her life, so I knew more lessons would be coming through the years for me and Triston.

I had Tracy flat iron Triston's hair. Lawrence was helping Jason downstairs and running messages between us. He had the biggest smile that whole day. He kept telling me for months that he wasn't going to let me trip, and now it was show time. I think he just wanted to be in front of all the people. He is not shy. I sat at the table for a while so Teah could do my eyelashes. Another letter came and a gift by way of Lawrence. It was a Pandora bracelet. Every time we were in the mall, I would point to a Pandora bracelet through the window and tell Jason, "I'm going to get me one of those bracelets one day." And now in my hands was my very own Pandora bracelet. The charm was a bride and groom, and the groom is dipping the bride. This was perfect because since I lost a hundred pounds I'd been having Jason dip me every chance I got.

Everything was coming together smoothly. The only thing I was worried about was the space downstairs. When the table and chairs arrived all the girls went downstairs and set everything up. They were rock stars. When I walked downstairs, I could do nothing but cry. The chairs were in rows of four and they made a walkway for us to get to the altar. Two wooden benches sat underneath the huge window. The curtain I had special ordered looked like ribbons of clouds in the sky. These curtains were extremely dramatic. Our vision was coming true. I was about to get married to the man I knew without a shadow of a doubt was put in my life by God. The Oklahoma Four / Fab Four were like my little fairy godmothers, here to help me through one of the most important days of my life. The air in my home was sweet and crisp. It was perfect.

I received two more letters from Jason but the last one did it in for me. I was getting ready and taking pictures with the photographer when Jason called. He told me to look underneath the chair in our room. Underneath was a letter. This letter was different. In this letter I felt his excitement, I felt his fears, I felt this man would die before anything or anyone would harm me. I felt this man's whole soul through this letter. I tried to clean myself before the photographer got the ugly cry. I was ready to go get my husband. I would never have to worry about love or family again. I trusted God. I let my family go and now I had blossomed into a woman, into Jason Williamson's wife, into a woman of God. Never in a million years would I have thought anything like this would be possible, but it really was happening.

I was all alone in the room. I could hear people going downstairs to take their seats. My son came into the room and smiled so big. "Mom are you ready?" This guy is so wise. He always tells me how proud he is of me. He tells me his hopes and dreams. All this is new for us. Lawrence and I were never that close. He was always around his dad and I was with Torri in the early years.

"Lawrence," I said, "before you walk me down the aisle, I want you to know how proud I am of you."

He looked up at me and said, "Mom, I'm proud of you. Now it's time to get you to J'Man." That was the nickname Lawrence had given to Jason.

Seeing Jason for the first time was breath-taking. I miss him so much that day. He truly is my best friend. Jason's suit fit him like a glove. It was navy blue, and his tie was a dusty pink. The shoes were a dark leather. His beard was trimmed a little lower and it connected to his fade. Everything went so well together.

The walk seemed to take forever but we finally reached Jason and his smile was so bright. Jason's vows were beautiful; he made just about everyone cry, including me. The officiant pronounced us as husband and wife, and Jason dipped me like I'd been making him do since June. I went upstairs and Jason went to work on transforming the downstairs into the area for dinner. The guest moved upstairs and the Oklahoma Four helped with the food and organizing where everyone should go. They were truly fairy godmothers that day. When I tell you God was in control. GOD WAS IN CONTROL! That wedding was beautiful. Everything went off without a hitch. I did forget my bouquet, but Tracy went upstairs and passed it to me. Other than that, everything was amazing.

The next day I got up early and made a big breakfast for the girls. We had a big day and we still had the reception to get ready for the following day. So, the wedding took place Thursday, and the reception was Saturday. Jason was doing his famous barbecue for everyone and he was extremely nervous. So, our Friday itinerary was like this: breakfast, site see, shopping, and back home to get all the food prepped for forty people. I was tired just thinking about everything, but I wanted the girls to see DC while they were here, and I promised Becky that she'd see the White house. That was the only thing she asked, and I was going to make it happen.

We loaded up two cars and took off for DC. With the COVID-19 we still had to wear a mask everywhere we went. Getting to the subway we had to go through the mall. Once everyone got out of the car Jason and the kids were in front and had pushed the elevator button. I ran to catch up with them and the girls were bringing up the rear. I jump on the elevator and Tracy said go ahead. I figured she wanted to wait because Rose was digging in her purse for, I didn't know what. We were at the bottom level and the elevator just sat. The kids and I started talking and walking around. Jason asked what happened to the girls. We laughed but I didn't understand what was taking them so long to get on the elevator. I went back upstairs, and they were all around Rose while she looked in her purse in the same spot where I left them.

"Hey guys!" I yelled. "What's going on?"

"Rose doesn't have her mask," Tracy stated. I was furious because for one everyone knows you have to have your mask on. Two, why did they feel they couldn't let me know that was the hold up? Three, I have disposable masks in the car. If people could commutate effectively then this issue could have been resolved a long time ago. I told them, which I'm sure came out very aggressively, "I have a mask in the car, let's go!" I then walked off by myself and retrieved the mask. I was so upset that it was four of them and they couldn't problem solve.

When I got back to Jason, I told him what happened, and we got outside right before the subway when someone stated they had to use the restroom. Ugh. I was just ready to go home at that point. We waited another fifteen minutes and finally everyone came out of the store.

"Listen," I said, "I don't want the rest of the day to go on with tension, so let's clear the air." I told them why I felt the way I did. I listened to them and understood how things could have been handled differently. Before we got on the subway things were back on track and I felt better. I hate having unresolved issues, and this was my weekend—come hell or high water I was going to be happy.

Site seeing was amazing. We got to see the White House and a few other attractions. We ate from the hotdog cart, which is always my favourite. I think it's because the movies make them look incredible. They never are, but I never learn. I uploaded pictures to social media and tagged the girls. When we got home, I went on Becky's social media page and she had pictures of herself in front of the White House and of herself at my wedding but that was it. I was confused. What was going on? I thought to myself. Is my friend ashamed of me? She liked black culture and was at my home with nothing but black people, yet she didn't post pictures with any of us. This was so upsetting to me. I began to cry because my friendship was not what I believed it to be. I knew she voted for Trump, but so did a lot of my friends.

I had an order to pick up and Tracy said she wanted to ride with me. Becky called out, "I got shot gun!" I became nervous for some reason. God was in control and I couldn't let anyone know I had just been crying.

Returning home, I asked the girls how they were enjoying their stay in Maryland. They both talked about different highlights. I somehow asked Becky if her family knew she was here. She answered vaguely, just, "Oh yeah, I told them I was going on a trip." I then asked whether she supported the BLM movement. Her face looked angry, and she whipped her head around and said, "They have some bad motives, so I don't agree with everything they stand for." Well, I got the answer I was looking for. I knew she was a Republican that didn't faze me. I think I am a Republican at times myself because of my own beliefs, but maybe God just wanted her to be around some people that did support BLM and could show her that were are not all bad, just like not all white Republicans are racists. I told her that I understood why she couldn't put pictures up on social media. Some family members wouldn't approve. This is the year 2020, and you must still watch who you interact with based on color. I was in shock, but I understood.

October 3rd was here and there was so much to do. Jason had been up since five a.m. cooking ribs. I had everything ready from the night before. The weather was very warm, which was surprising for this time of the year. I couldn't help but smile and looked up to the sky and say thank You, God. I couldn't believe how great everything turned out. All my life my mother had the idea that things never worked out, so that's what I always believed: that things couldn't go well for long periods of time because we were destined to fail. Maybe this is why I never tried in life, because I knew, or I was led to believe, that things would eventually fail, which placed a "What's the point in trying?" attitude in my mind. When God showed me a glimpsed of what he had in store for me, He focused a lot on Triston. How he told me she was just like me and that I needed to start setting an example for her, holding myself to a higher standard. I had the power to control the outcome not only for this party but the outcome of my life. And she had the same power for her life as well.

The reception was lovely. I got to meet the rest of Jason's family. His brother Spanky was a lot shorter than I had pictured. He was over fifty and looked like an old pimp. He looked at me and said, "Do you know who I am?"

I said, "Spanky," with a confused look on my face.

Jason and I had our first dance as husband and wife, and it felt like no one was around. "We did it," Jason whispered in my ear. He had a tear coming down his check. His eyes sparkled as tiny stars dripped down.

"Yes," I said, "we are married." I think it just finally hit both of us that we were forever, and that felt amazing. The song that played was the same one I walked down the aisle to. "Forever" by Jason Nelson. Such an amazing song.

The night finally wound down, and I was not trying to clean anything that night. Everyone was exhausted and went right to bed. Jason and I couldn't wait for things to get back to normal around the house. But what was that going to feel like? I remember smiling just thinking what God had in store for me.

The morning came faster than I wanted, and I needed to get the girls to the airport. I told them because they had been like godmothers, they didn't have to get me a wedding gift. They looked shocked; I don't think they were going to get me a gift anyway. It didn't matter—they did more than enough. Jason made sure he could fit them all in one car because he did not want to make that drive to the airport again. I didn't blame him. He had put up with so much from my friends and family. He needed time to himself. The girls and I headed out and, in the car, laughed about some of the moments Rose had on the dance floor. On the drive back home, I just couldn't believe a Fitbit I bought in 2015 got me to move over 1200 miles away. I found my voice and stood up to my family and I'm not going to let anything hold me back. Because of Fitbit, I was finally able to accept the gift God has given me, and most importantly, I'm finally happy.

Tiffany and Torri walking

Torri playing the keyboard

Torri and Triston

Father and Daughter Dance Torri and Lambert

Triston the Anime artist

Me Vs. Me

Before and After

First Text Message

Torri and Lawrence

Torri and Triston

#FitToBeWilliamson

CPSIA information can be obtained
at www.ICGtesting.com
Printed in the USA
BVHW061522020721
611053BV00022B/1649